Ed Sheeran

PIANO
VOCAL
GUITAR

2	THE A TEAM
7	DRUNK
13	UNI
21	GRADE 8
27	WAKE ME UP
35	SMALL BUMP
42	THIS
45	THE CITY
51	LEGO HOUSE
58	YOU NEED ME, I DON'T NEED YOU
66	KISS ME
73	GIVE ME LOVE

ISBN 978-1-4803-4451-8

HAL•LEONARD®
CORPORATION
7777 W. BLUEMOUND RD. P.O. BOX 13819 MILWAUKEE, WI 53213

Visit Hal Leonard Online at
www.halleonard.com

THE A TEAM

Words and Music by
ED SHEERAN

DRUNK

Words and Music by ED SHEERAN
and JAKE GOSLING

Moderate beat

I wan-na be drunk when I wake up, on the right _ side of the wrong _
I wan-na hold your heart in both hands, not watch it fiz-zle at the bot-tom of a Coke can. _

___ bed and nev-er an ex-cuse I made up. Tell _ you the truth, I did what
___ And I got no plans for the week-end, so should we speak then? Keep it be-tween friends,

did-n't kill me,____ it nev - er made _ me strong - er ____ at all. __
though I know you'll nev - er love me like __ you used _____ to. ____

Love will scar your make - up.
There may be oth - er peo-ple like us

Lips sticks to me,__ so now I may-be lean
who see the flick - er of a clip-per when they light _ up.

back there, I'm sat here wish-ing I ___ was so - ber. ____
Flames just cre - ate us, but burns don't ____ heal like __ be - fore.

UNI

Words and Music by ED SHEERAN
and JAKE GOSLING

Hmm. ____ I found your hair band on my bed-room _ floor.

The on-ly ev-i-dence that you've been here be-fore. And I don't get waves of

miss-ing you an-y-more. They're more like tsu-na-mi tides in my eyes. Nev-er

Recorded a half step higher.

18

GRADE 8

Words and Music by ED SHEERAN,
ROBERT CONLON and SUKHDEEP UPPAL

Moderate groove

My mind is a war-ri-or, my heart is a for-eign-er.

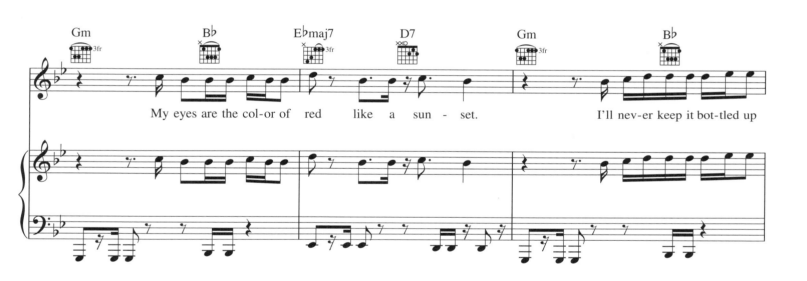

My eyes are the col-or of red like a sun - set. I'll nev-er keep it bot-tled up

and left to the hands of the co-ro-ner. Be a true heart, not a fol-low-er, we're not done yet. __

To Coda ⊕

26

WAKE ME UP

Words and Music by ED SHEERAN
and JAKE GOSLING

D

E

D.S. al Coda

till I fall a-sleep, and flut-ter eye-lash on my cheek be-tween _ the sheets. _

CODA

A

And I think you hate the smell of smoke, you al-ways try get me to stop.

D

E

You drink as much as me, and I get drunk _ a lot.

A

D

So, I take you to the beach and walk a-long the sand. _____ And I'll make you a heart pen-dant

SMALL BUMP

Words and Music by
ED SHEERAN

THIS

Words and Music by ED SHEERAN
and GORDON MILLS

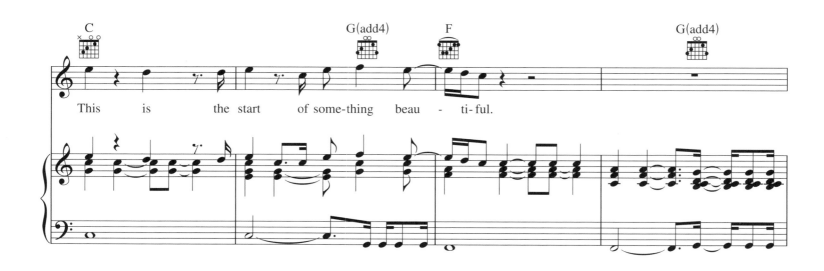

This is the start of some-thing beau - ti-ful.

This is the start of some-thing new. ___ And

THE CITY

Words and Music by ED SHEERAN
and JAKE GOSLING

Moderate groove

This ci-ty nev-er ____ sleeps. ____
The pave-ment is ___ my ___ friend, ___

I hear the peo-ple walk by when it's ___ late. ____
it will take me where __ I need to go. ____

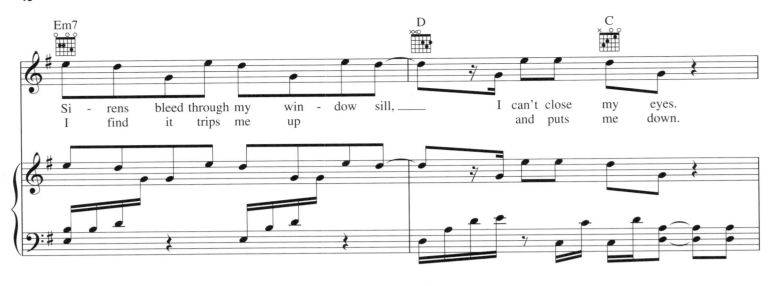

Si - rens bleed through my win - dow sill, ____ I can't close my eyes.
I find it trips me up and puts me down.

Don't con - trol what I'm in - to. ____
This is not what I'm used to. ____

This is tow - er is ____ a - live.
And the shop a - cross ____ the road

the lights that blind keep me a - wake. _____
ful - fils my needs and gives me com-pan - y when I need it.

Hood up and lace un - tied, _____ sleep fills my mind.
Voic - es speak through my walls, _____ I don't think I'm gon-na make it

Can't con - trol what I'm in - to. _____
past to - mor - row. _____

LEGO HOUSE

Words and Music by ED SHEERAN,
CHRIS LEONARD and JAKE GOSLING

With a driving beat

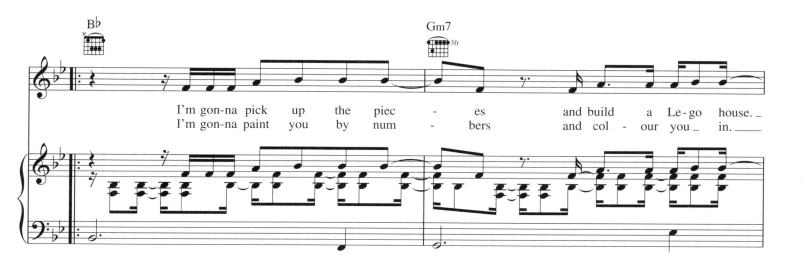

I'm gon-na pick up the piec - es and build a Le-go house.
I'm gon-na paint you by num - bers and col - our you in.

If things go wrong, we can knock it down.
If things go right, we can frame it and put you on a wall.

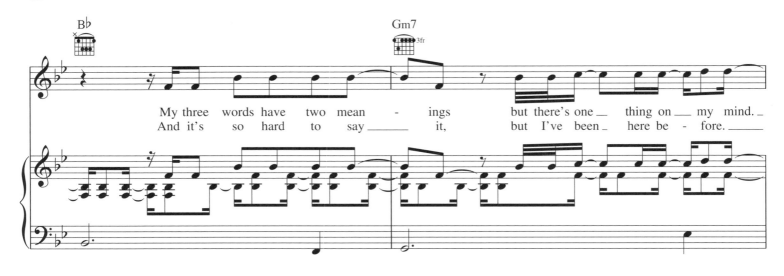

My three words have two mean - ings, but there's one __ thing on __ my mind.
And it's so hard to say _____ it, but I've been __ here be - fore. _____

_____ It's all for _____ you, _ mm. _____
_____ Now I'll sur-ren - der up my heart _____ and swap it for yours. __

And it's dark in a cold De-cem - ber, but I've got you to keep me warm. _

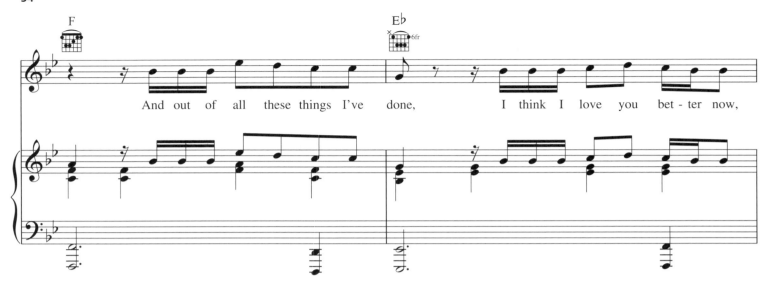

And out of all these things I've done, I think I love you bet-ter now,

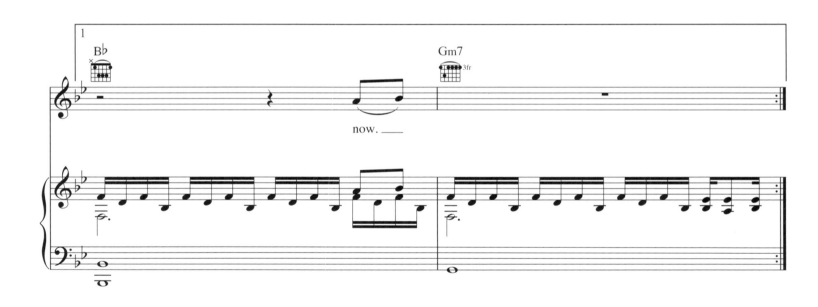

now. ____

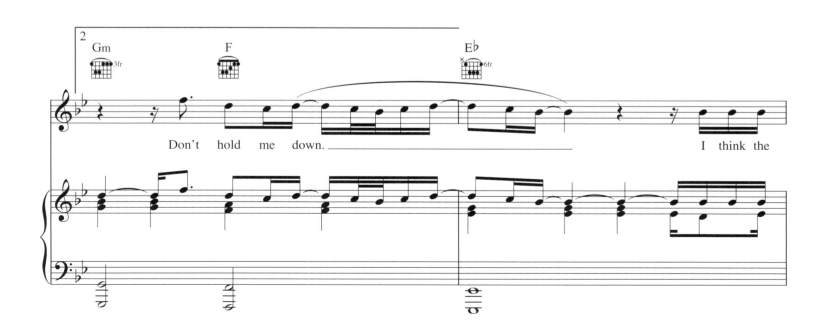

Don't hold me down. ____ I think the

brac - es are break - ing _____ and it's more than I _____ can take. _____

And it's dark in a cold De-cem - ber, but I've got you to keep me warm. _

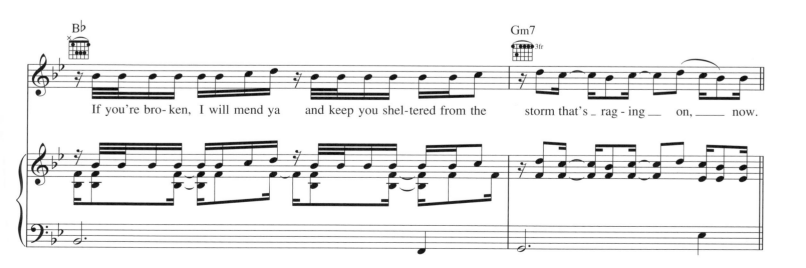

If you're bro-ken, I will mend ya and keep you shel-tered from the storm that's _ rag - ing _____ on, _____ now.

I'm out of touch, I'm out of love. I'll pick you up when you're get-ting down.

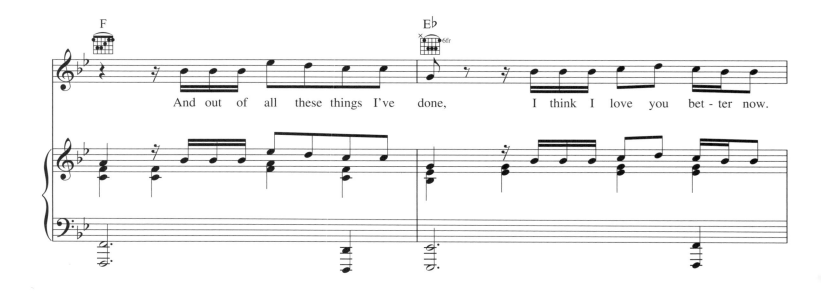

And out of all these things I've done, I think I love you bet-ter now.

I'm out of sight, I'm out of mind. I'll do it all for you in time.

And out of all these things I've done, I think I love you bet-ter now.

I'm out of touch, I'm out of love. I'll pick you up when you're get-ting down.

And out of all these things I've done, I will love you bet-ter now.

YOU NEED ME
I DON'T NEED YOU

Words and Music by
ED SHEERAN

Em

you.   You need me,___ man, I don't need   you.   You need me,___ man, I don't need

G6

To Coda ⊕

Asus

you.   You need me,___ man, I don't need   you at all. You need me.___   I sing, I

Cmaj7   **D**

Em

write my own tune and I write my own verse;   hell,___ don't need an-oth-er word-smith to make my tune sell.
And I won't be   a pro-duct of my gen-re.   My___ mind will___ al-ways be strong-er, like my songs are.

G6

Asus

Call your-self a sing-er-writ-er? You're just bluff-in'. Name's on the cred-its and you did-n't write noth-in'.
Nev-er be-lieve the bull-shit that fake guys feed to you. Al-ways read the sto-ries that you hear on Wi-ki-pe-di-a.

Cmaj7   **D**

KISS ME

Words and Music by ED SHEERAN,
JULIE FROST, JUSTIN FRANKS
and ERNEST WILSON

Moderately slow

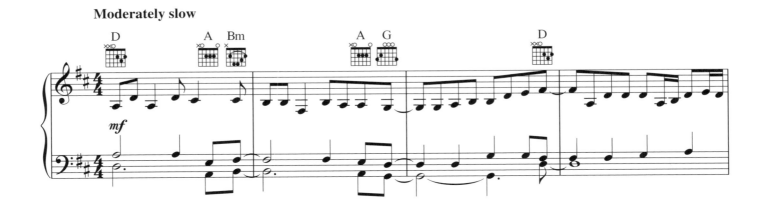

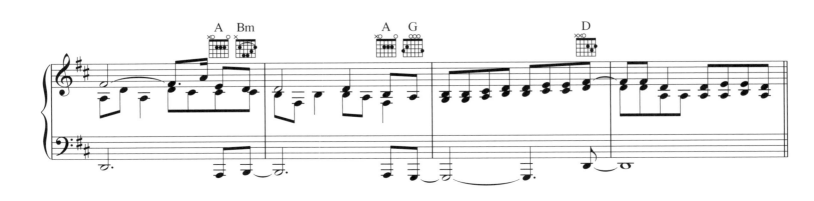

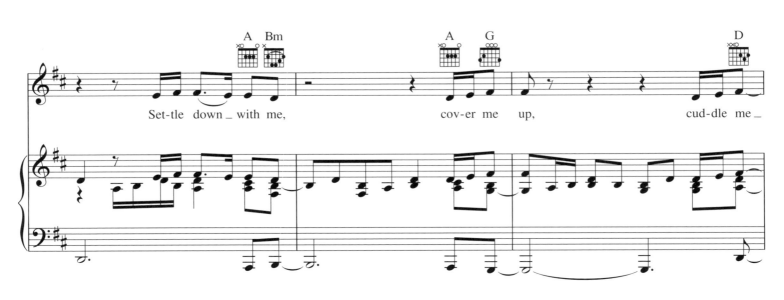

loved,   you wan - na be _____ loved.

This   feels _____ like fall - ing in _____ love, _____   fall - ing in

love,   fall-ing in love. __

GIVE ME LOVE

Words and Music by ED SHEERAN,
CHRIS LEONARD and JAKE GOSLING

Moderately, in 2

Give me love, like her.

Recorded a half step higher.